JUST KEEP PEDALING

Publishing & Promotions

DR. SYLVIA COLE

CALLED 2 INSPIRE, LLC
PUBLISHING & PROMOTIONS
Book & Magazine Publishing
P.O. BOX 680541
Houston, Texas 77268

JUST KEEP PEDALING

Copyright 2024 © Dr. Sylvia Cole

All rights reserved. No parts of this book may be reproduced or transmitted in any form without written permission from the author.

ISBN: 9798325583537

DEDICATION

To you, dear reader, may you find inspiration and empowerment within these pages to move forward and JUST KEEP PEDALING when life has other plans.

~Dr. Sylvia Cole~

"No matter what happens or how bad it seems, life does go on, and it will be better tomorrow."

~Dr. Maya Angelou~

What Others Are Saying About
JUST KEEP PEDALING
By
Dr. Sylvia Cole

The year 2023 was very difficult for me. So often I felt stuck. THIS book is just what I needed. Dr. Sylvia is very authentic and relatable in sharing her message. If you are feeling stuck too no matter what you have faced or may be facing now, THIS book is your answer.

~Dennis C. (New York)

This book is empowering and definitely inspiring. JUST KEEP PEDALING is a testament to how one can move forward and still fulfill your goals and dreams no matter the "vicissitudes of life" you experience. Thanks Dr. Sylvia for this masterpiece which I am confident will change lives.

~Dr. J. Baker (Texas)

I really loved reading this book. As a high school student, I often feel like giving up when things change or don't go as I would prefer. This book is a great motivator and I will share it with my classmates too.

~Melissa G. (Mississippi)

After reading this book, I now understand life is choice-driven. I must choose to move forward in the midst of life's uncertainty. What truly hit home for me is the never stop dreaming message by Dr. Sylvia. For so long, I felt like my dreams died. I am now more determined than ever after reading this book to keep believing and keep dreaming so I can be a blessing to my family and encourage others along the way too. POWERFUL READ by Dr. Sylvia who is an exceptional, inspiring writer!

~Kevin G. (Chicago)

I truly know why THIS book is a #1 Best-Seller. THIS book is definitely a must-read. It is an awesome reminder to never give up no matter what you face in life. Dr. Sylvia also provides practical strategies for implementing the steps so that you can move

forward when life has other plans. Thanks Dr. Sylvia for your insight and wisdom which I am confident will inspire and bless millions.

~Rachel T. (Utah)

This book can help you in every life situation. I am in my second year of college and this book has inspired me to keep going no matter what. Dr. Sylvia is a great motivator also.

~Reggie B. (Florida)

WOW! After reading this book, I am so encouraged and ready to reclaim my life. I am facing some challenges now but life is not over. During my difficult times, I often forget to be grateful. As Dr. Sylvia so eloquently shared, gratitude is a mindset. I truly needed a plan for moving forward and this phenomenal author truly gave me what I needed. I will also share this #1 Best-Seller with my family and friends.

~Michael C. (California)

ACKNOWLEDGMENTS

I remain grateful to God for blessing me with the gifts of speaking and writing. I will continue to please Him with my life and *INSPIRE OTHERS TO GREATNESS*!

To my beautiful and loving mother Artharene: Thank you for your unconditional love and wisdom and raising me with a God-consciousness.
You are my #1 fan and supporter and for this I am forever grateful. I love you more than you will ever know. I also remember my father, Otis, with much love and fond memories.

To my siblings: Shirley (Ralph), Denise, Randall, and Darrell (Monica): Each of you remain very precious and special to me. We are a team and when one of us wins, we ALL win! I also remember my dear brothers Robert, LeNard, and Sheldon with much love. I miss each of you dearly.

To my nieces and nephews: Each of you are very special to me and hold a unique place in my life.

To Mrs. Virgie Brown, my fifth-grade teacher: Thank you for recognizing my passion for speaking and creating opportunities for me to display this gift. You also gave me a love for English. I am grateful to God for his Amazing Grace and I cherish our weekly conversations.

My gratitude extends to the following persons for taking the time to write a Testimonial as to how this book impacted and inspired them in some way: Dennis C., Dr. J. Baker; Melissa G., Kevin G., Rachel T., Reggie B., and Michael C.

Finally, I am deeply appreciative for the connections I have made with so many amazing people across the world and for all who have told me I have inspired, uplifted, and empowered them to take action. I remain excited about,

INSPIRING OTHERS TO GREATNESS!

Just Keep Pedaling

CONTENTS

Introduction……………………………………………………1

Chapter 1: Stay Grateful………………………………9

Chapter 2: Accept Where You Are……………13

Chapter 3: Don't Forget Your "Why"…………17

Chapter 4: Learn From Your Mistakes………21

Chapter 5: Reset…………………………………………23

Chapter 6: Invest in Yourself……………………25

Chapter 7: Take Action!……………………………27

Conclusion………………………………………………29

Call To Action…………………………………………30

Inspiring Life Quotes for Moving Forward………31

Meet Dr. Sylvia………………………………………34

Connect With Dr. Sylvia…………………………37

JUST KEEP PEDALING

INTRODUCTION

JUST KEEP PEDALING! I will never forget these three words my mother always said to me when she was teaching me to ride a bicycle. Sometimes I was unable to stay straight on the seat, sometimes one foot would fall off the pedal, sometimes the bike would go from side to side, and sometimes I would actually fall off the bike. She would say at every angle: JUST KEEP PEDALING!

As I reflect on this childhood experience, I understand how much it relates to the vicissitudes of life. An automobile accident, losing a loved one, an unexpected health challenge, job loss, or even being called to jury duty are examples of the vicissitudes of life. I firmly believe that most would say they would rather avoid them and not go through them. Some persons have more vicissitudes of life than others but it is so true that no one can escape life events that challenge and test us.

Hence, this is how this book title, JUST KEEP PEDALING came about. I was so excited about my dreams and visions for 2023. My vision board was complete and I was overjoyed and in high anticipation as to how God would favor me and open doors that no man could close. But little did I know that life had other plans. As I reflect on the year 2023, it was definitely full of the vicissitudes of life. It started off with having thousands of dollars stolen from me, followed by closed doors, betrayal, and a health challenge while being the caregiver for my elderly mother and sister (I am honored to serve them). But through it all, I never forgot my mother's words, JUST KEEP PEDALING. I never felt like giving up. I understood that 2023 was just a season and a part of my story. The latter part of 2023 I had new open doors and opportunities presented to me and God is continuously opening doors of opportunity I never saw coming. He's just that kind of God!

You too may be in a season where you are facing vicissitudes of life that perhaps have left you shaken to the core and perhaps made you wonder

why your dreams have been delayed or if your dreams and desires of your heart will ever be fulfilled. I say to you what my mother told me, JUST KEEP PEDALING. God is faithful!

Life is not over. Delay is not denial. It may at times look like the sun will not shine anymore in your life. I know that it will shine again for you just like it is for me. Stay positive and focused. Keep believing and dreaming. Speak the Word of God over your situation. No matter the vicissitude of life you face, implement these 7 Steps For Moving Forward When Life Has Other Plans and,

JUST KEEP PEDALING!

~DR. SYLVIA COLE~
CEO – CALLED 2 INSPIRE, LLC
Best-Selling Author
International Best-Selling Author
University Professor
Book & Magazine Publisher
Empowerment Speaker
Podcast Host
KYOK Radio Host
Presidential Lifetime Achievement Award Recipient

Just Keep Pedaling

Count your blessings!

Chapter One
STAY GRATEFUL

"Do not spoil what you have by desiring what you have not; remember that what you now have was once among the things you only hoped for."

Staying grateful is so vital for moving forward when life has other plans. Life is not absent of stress and uncertainty for any of us. I am so thankful that my mom taught my siblings and me as little children to always be grateful. Gratefulness is about appreciating your life, loved ones and never feeling like you have to compare yourself to anyone. Moving forward can be difficult for those who may perhaps see someone in their circle succeeding and they are stuck and still waiting for that one door to open, that one phone call or a dream to finally come to pass. But do not let this stop you from moving forward. We are all in the race of life but running our own race. I remember a quote that says: "life is a race and what matters most isn't when a person crosses the finish line, but how strong they've grown along the way. As you wait in the race and keep moving, you will have the strength to keep going toward the finish line no matter what comes your way.

Don't be discouraged when things are not looking on the bright side. Remember, after the rain, the sunshine returns. Remain grateful and do not get distracted or off focus from the things that really matter. You are not the only person in the world dealing with vicissitudes of life.

I remember many years ago meeting a friend of a relative who faced one challenge after another. Whenever she shares her story, she always says, "I was sick and tired of being sick and tired but I knew life was not over for me in spite of my situation. I chose to remain grateful and hopeful."

This is so true. There is no such thing as a perfect life no matter our race, educational level, financial status, resume, or zip code. I have always enjoyed riding roller coasters. It gives me an opportunity to display courage and also explore my competitive side. I am absolutely thrilled because although one may be facing a vicissitude of life, you can for a moment experience a joy that makes you laugh in the midst of your despair.

You are probably asking: Dr. Sylvia, how can I remain grateful thru the vicissitudes of life? I have an answer for you:

(1) Reach out to others who you know are dealing with a life situation. Offer a word of encouragement letting them know they are in your thoughts and prayers.
(2) Keep a journal and document what you are grateful for on a daily basis
(3) Record your successes no matter how small they may appear to be. "Find gratitude in the little things and your well of gratitude will never run dry."
(4) Encourage your Social Media audience with a positive post. You will find someone who needed to see just what you posted.

Hence, I believe staying grateful is a mindset that you must choose as you are enduring the vicissitudes of life. Count your blessings!

The reality is that life does not go as we have planned it.

Chapter Two
ACCEPT WHERE YOU ARE

"God grant me serenity to accept the things I cannot change, courage to change the things I can and the wisdom to know the difference."

Acceptance in difficult life situations can be challenging but is crucial for emotional well-being. The reality is that life does not always go as we have planned it. We can have a perfect day planned and what do you know: a child wakes up sick, a parent has a medical emergency, you have a flat tire, etc. Many times we tend to hold on with the life we planned and what we really want even when nothing is working out towards that plan. I remember wanting something so badly that I jumped on the opportunity. I later realized it was a door that I opened and not God. It was a process to close the door but favor showed up and a bigger and better door opened.

I am a person who loves quotes because I enjoy hearing the stories and perspectives of others. As I reflect on the subtitle for this book, When life Has Other Plans, I reflect on things I have heard others say thru the years:

I would have been living in another state if I had married my college sweetheart instead of my current husband.

I would have finished medical school if my dad had not passed and I had to move back home.

I would have been much further in life had I not been a teenage mom or dad.

I would have still been at the same company if I had gotten that much-deserved promotion.

"Start by acknowledging your feelings without judgment. Reflect on what you can control and what you cannot. Focus on small steps and celebrate any progress, no matter how minor. Practice self-compassion and understand that it is

okay not to have all the answers. I love what Best-Selling Author Steve Maraboli says: "Incredible change happens in your life when you decide to take control of what you do have power over instead of craving control over what you don't." You must never forget that acceptance does not mean that you are giving up; instead it is about finding peace in the midst of the vicissitudes of life.

You can truly have fun when you are living in purpose.

Chapter Three
DON'T FORGET YOUR "WHY"

Oprah Winfrey once said "There's no greater gift than to honor your life's calling. It's why you were born. And how you become truly alive." I agree. I also understand it is crucial to always have a reason for doing things. I remember my mother telling me as a teenager always to be able to explain why you are doing something. I must admit, I did not fully comprehend or deem it important at the time, but my "WHY" would play the most crucial factor in my decision-making on the path to finding purpose as well as moving forward.

You must not forget your "WHY" for several reasons. First, your "WHY" is the determining factor in whether you will or will not participate in certain activities, go to lunch with someone, and more than anything it keeps you focused on your goals thereby alleviating any distractions. Second, your "WHY" fuels your passion. It pushes you beyond ordinary and potentially doing something extraordinary that guides your decision-making. Third, your "WHY" plays a crucial part in goal-setting and allows you to focus on living a life based on values even when life has other plans. Values also keep you from potentially detouring on your path to purpose. Also, I have found that when you know your purpose or find your purpose in life, it is then you can live a life of integrity. One of the things very important to me is being on time and always doing things in a timely manner. One of the things that others can say if asked about me is that Dr. Cole is going to be on time. I must say this is a trait I picked up from my mother and grandparents. They believed in being on time, but I did not know how it would affect my life and integrity until I truly started operating in purpose. Lastly, one of the things that I truly love about remembering your "WHY" is it makes life so enjoyable. You can truly have fun when you are living in purpose, even when facing vicissitudes of life. I am enjoying every second of living a purpose-driven life even when things do not go as

planned. I wake up every morning excited about the goals I have set because of living in purpose, and YOU can too. Don't forget your "WHY!"

Growth is not always comfortable, but necessary.

Chapter Four
LEARN FROM YOUR MISTAKES

Life is comprised of good choices and bad choices, ups and downs, and successes and mistakes. You may have heard of the saying that "what doesn't kill you makes you stronger." I witness that there are things that you will endure you will realize after the fact it made you stronger. I recall an incident with a former student many years ago. This student played around the entire year and failed his current grade. His parents decided to let him learn from his failures and did not allow him to go to summer school which would have allowed him to advance to the next grade level along with his peers. This student said that this was one of the best decisions his parents could have made, although he did not see it at the time. He is now in his thirties and working as an attorney in a major city. This truly helped him during his path to purpose and moving forward.

I am sure that you can also look back over your life at those times where we experienced mistakes and reflect on how they helped you and made you stronger, wiser, and perhaps pushed us into purpose. I definitely know that I learned from my experiences of 2023 even though they were not a part of my plan. A dear friend often reflects that, "there is a lesson and a blessing in everything we go through." When you make mistakes, it is not comfortable. Growth Is not always comfortable but necessary.

Additionally, learning from our mistakes also teaches us how to handle disappointment. In this life, you will have many disappointments. None of us makes it through life without disappointment. Life is full of obstacles and challenging times.

The bible reminds us: "In this world you will have tribulation, but be of good cheer, I have overcome the world." (John 16:33)

When you truly understand that disappointments are a part of life, I often say that "one can be content even in the face of adversity. You should

not begin to feel that you are entitled or have the expectation that you are free from mistakes because we "all fall short of His glory."

All habits are not good habits.

Chapter Five
RESET

"I am not a product of my circumstances. I am a product of my decisions."

Have you ever been in a situation where you absolutely looked forward to a vacation or time off after it was over? You probably thought like me, "A vacation is just what I need after this turbulent time." I felt this way after so many unexpected disruptions in my life in 2023. I had to focus on my next after these unexpected blows. I had to decide on a course of action. I was working and serving others relentlessly prior to this setback. I thought, "Not now." But it was RESET time.

No matter the vicissitude of life you face, a reset is necessary. It may be a financial disaster, health challenge, or even a family situation but you can move forward. Perhaps you know you just need a new start or a change in direction maybe due to feeling overwhelmed with life and just plain frustrated. To reset means "to set again or moving forward differently." Here are some ways you can reset and begin to move forward:

(1) Think about what is most important to you or in other words, What is your priority? What is most important to you now? You know that change is necessary. Focus on what you can control and

always bear in mind that life can happen at any moment for all of us.

(2) Check what you are doing that is viewed as habitual. All of us have habits. We may not think about them often because they are just what we do. All habits are not good habits. Habits are not always huge and just need to work for us.

(3) Work on developing a healthy mindset. I have always understood that mindset is so key because of how I was raised. You need a proper mindset for your reset. I recently took a Masterclass and meditation was discussed and demonstrated. It was powerful. This is but one thing you can partake in towards developing a positive mindset. Journaling on a daily basis is also great. This will also allow you to not only record your thoughts daily but give you a record to reflect on how far you have come and grown, Hey, Start Journaling!

Remember the words of Richie Norton: "Every sunset is an opportunity to reset. Every sunrise begins with new eyes."

Chapter Six
INVEST IN YOURSELF

"Invest in yourself. It's like being a boxer; you've got to be in training so that when the bell rings, you get your direction and you come out of the corner and you are ready."

I must first say to you that YOU matter as YOU move forward. YOU are important! YOU are valued! Warren Buffet reminded us that, "The best investment you will ever make will be on yourself." I firmly believe that each of us has a responsibility to take care of ourselves. This will allow us to provide our energy and quality time to other relationships. I personally believe that when I invest in myself I definitely get a return on this investment. So, I pose the question. How will YOU invest in YOU?

Investing in yourself is so much more than how you handle your finances. This also entails taking care of yourself spiritually, emotionally, and physically.

How will you focus on growing and developing personally? Personally, I am intentional about learning and growing whether I am having a challenging time or whether all is well. The reality is you cannot get today back and I have learned to live life with absolutely no regrets. Do I wish I could have perhaps done some things differently? Absolutely! Do I wish I could have responded to something or someone differently? Absolutely! There is not a do-over. So make the most of today.

You may waste time. But effort is one thing that is never wasted. So put forth your best effort. You will find that as you invest in yourself, you will learn valuable skills that will help you n so many areas of your life. I recently attended a masterclass that had nothing to do with writing or speaking but I learned some valuable strategies and tools for my business and you can do the same. By the way, I made some great new connections as well.

Investing in yourself via your time, energy and resources is crucial to moving forward when life does not go as planned. Make a decision that you will not only invest in yourself in challenging times but it will be an ongoing process. I make it a point to read or learn something new on a daily basis. I love what Ghandhi says: "Live as if you were to die tomorrow. Learn as if you were to live forever."

Chapter Seven
TAKE ACTION

"To achieve greatness, start where you are, use what you have, and do what you can."

When life does not go as planned, it is imperative that we TAKE ACTION to move forward. I have learned that in life we can devise what we may think is a perfect plan. But at any moment life can take a drastic turn and we face a situation we never saw coming. I did not anticipate having to be a caregiver to two people simultaneously nor did I expect to have a health challenge in the midst of caregiving. Perhaps you did not expect to get laid off from your high paying corporate child as a single parent and paying college tuition. You did not expect your child to get in serious legal trouble after hanging with the wrong crowd although he or she is being raised in a Christian home. We did not expect a global pandemic that would shut down our nation and change how we do business.

When our life is interrupted and our goals and dreams appear to be shattered and are placed on hold, we can still move forward by adjusting our goals and plans. We may face fear and perhaps allow the fear of the unknown to shake us at times. Again, delay is not denial. You must remain excited about your future. When I was in a place where my life did not go as planned, I had to drastically change my schedule and do business differently. I understood the importance of staying connected to God and staying in faith. I continued to start my day off in the secret place with God. I was definitely in a different season. A spiritual sister would often send me encouraging words and remind me that God has not forgotten about the dreams and desires of my heart. I never stopped dreaming. I never stopped believing. I never stopped speaking the Word of God over my life. I often meditated on the first commandment with a promise noted in Exodus 20:12: "Honor thy mother and thy father that it may be well with thee and you may live long on the earth." Caregiving is one of the ways we honor our parents.

However, there is no one way for move forward when life does not go as planned. But I know what has worked for me and I am now teaching others to do the same. But I also know that an array of emotions is normal, and they may also change over time. You must not be consumed with emotions where you are unable to move forward. I have heard countless others talk about being so uncertain about the future as a result of the pandemic. I often say in one of my other books: The music changed and we must dance differently. This same thing is true now as you are facing your situation. You too must dance differently because the music has changed.

Ask yourself what you learned from the situation. How do you envision moving forward and what does it look like for you? We cannot change everything but we can change our approach, Again, we must accept what we cannot change, have the courage to change the things we can and the wisdom to know the difference.

All of us will have seasons where life does not go as planned.

CONCLUSION

All of us will have seasons where life has other plans. We do not always know when we will face roadblocks in life that will derail our vision board. I often share that life is about perspective, so you must CHANGE YOUR PERSPECTIVE. You must change the way you see things when life does not go as planned. Try to reframe from developing a "why me" mentality or even becoming angry.

When life did not go as planned for me in 2023, I chose to embrace the season I was in and do the following and You must do the same:

Stay Grateful
Accept Where You Are
Don't Forget Your "Why"
Learn From Your Mistakes
Reset
Invest in Yourself
Take Action

You must know that life is not over for you. Your dreams will come to pass. Keep believing! Stay in Faith! Keep Trusting God! Keep speaking the Word of God over your situation. He won't fail you! Just as He is showing up and out for me, He will do the same for you. When life has other plans, **JUST KEEP PEDALING!**

CALL TO ACTION

SUBSCRIBE to my Podcast, JUST KEEP PEDALING with DR. SYLVIA on YouTube at:

@justkeeppedalingwithdrsylvia

SIGN-UP for my MASTERCLASS
SUCCESS and INSPIRING OTHERS TO GREATNESS

Visit: Justkeeppedaling.net

INSPIRING QUOTES
FOR
MOVING FORWARD IN LIFE

"Life is like riding a bicycle, to keep your balance, you must keep moving."

~Albert Einstein

"Stay committed to your decisions but stay flexible in your approach."

~Tony Robbins

"It's only after you've stepped outside your comfort zone that you begin to change, grow, and transform."

~Roy T. Bennett

"We keep moving forward, opening new doors, and doing new things, because we're curious and curiosity keeps leading us down new paths."

~Walt Disney

"If we fail to adapt, we fail to move forward."

~John Wooden

"It doesn't matter how many times you fall as long as you keep getting back up."
~Tyler Perry

"Do not judge me by my success, judge me by how many times I fell down and got back up again."
~Nelson Mandela

"Nothing happens until you decide. Make a decision and watch your life move forward."
~Oprah Winfrey

"Never make a permanent decision based on a temporary storm. No matter how raging the billows are today, remind yourself: "This too shall pass!"
~T.D. Jakes

"Keep moving forward, being your best, living with determination and faith."
~Joel Osteen

"Things happen along the way in our path. Instead of looking at it as a wall that's being put up in front of us, look at it as opportunity to scale new heights and to climb that wall – to see and do things you didn't think you were capable of."

~Robin Roberts

"Continue to strive. Continue to have goals. Continue to progress."

~Denzel Washington

"No matter how much falls on us, we keep plowing ahead. That's the only way to keep the roads clear."

~Greg Kincaid

'If you can't fly then run, if you can't run then walk, if you can't walk then crawl, but whatever you do you have to keep moving forward."

~Martin Luther King, Jr.

🎤 *Just Keep Pedaling* 🎤

MEET DR. SYLVIA COLE

Dr. Sylvia Cole (affectionately referred to as Dr. Sylvia) is an inspiring and captivating Motivational Speaker, KYOK Radio Personality, Host of the JUST KEEP PEDALING Podcast, Speaker Development Coach, #1 Best-Selling Author, International Best-Selling Author, Success Life Coach, University Professor, Magazine Publisher, Event Host, and Book Writing Coach/Publisher. She has been featured in several media outlets including FOX, CBS, and NBC News as well as Voyage Magazine, Women of Dignity Magazine, Jackson Daily News (Mississippi), and Making Headline News (Dallas, Texas). She has been recognized as a Rising Leader, one of the World's TOP 20 Christian Coaches by Divine Purpose Magazine, in the TOP 100 Influential Women in Business by The Herpreneur Magazine, Top Boss Women in 2022 by Power Conversations Magazine, nominated for the 2022 Emerging Leader of The Year Award by POWER UP SUMMIT, and in December 2022, Dr. Cole received the

Dr. Sylvia Cole

Presidential Lifetime Achievement Award for her service to the community.

Dr. Sylvia has been speaking and writing since the age of five when her mother and maternal grandmother realized she has been blessed with the gift of speaking. As a result, her maternal grandmother started taking her around their community to speak at churches and other events.

As the CEO of CALLED 2 INSPIRE, LLC Dr. Sylvia has a unique ability to captivate her audience through her storytelling and impeccable wisdom and charisma. She also empowers primarily women to live a life of purpose and implement specific principles for NEXT LEVEL success. Dr. Sylvia also helps others write, publish, and monetize their books and magazines.

Dr. Sylvia is also committed to impacting the lives of students and travels the country delivering her signature speech in school systems, Finding Purpose, based on her book *A Teen's GPS For Finding Life's Purpose*. Her book which is an Amazon #1 Best-Seller entitled, *When the Music Changes: A Parent's Guide to Help Students Succeed in A Pandemic*, is resonating with parents, teachers, students, and administrators across the country.

Another best-seller by Dr. Sylvia, *It Matters How You Play: A Guide for Next Level Success*, released in August 2022, is resonating with individuals, schools, businesses, and corporations across our nation.

Dr. Sylvia's best-selling book entitled, I Take God At His Word: How To Trust Him When You Can't Trace Him was released in November 2022.

Dr. Sylvia passionately believes that those who are bold enough to go after all God has for them are the ones who can impact the lives of others. She continues to share her platform and lift others as God elevates her. This Empowered Woman is on a mission to help build the kingdom and empower and serve others.

CONNECT WITH DR. SYLVIA

Facebook:
Dr-Sylvia Cole

Instagram:
Dr-Sylvia Cole

Twitter:
Dr-Sylvia Cole

YouTube:
@justkeeppedalingwithdrsylvia

Website:
justkeeppedaling.net

CALLED 2 INSPIRE

Made in the USA
Columbia, SC
24 June 2024